T0208834

WOMAN OF GOD:
WHAT IS YOUR REPORT?

W. R. Coleman

authorHOUSE®

AuthorHouse™
1663 Liberty Drive
Bloomington, IN 47403
www.authorhouse.com
Phone: 1 (800) 839-8640

Published by AuthorHouse 02/18/2019

ISBN: 978-1-7283-0088-7 (sc)
ISBN: 978-1-7283-0087-0 (e)

Library of Congress Control Number: 2019901959

WRITTEN BY ANOINTED
WOMEN OF GOD

Victoria C. Howard ~ Shabra C. Goodman
Monica Sargent ~ Mamie C. Thompson
Felicia Reed-Taylor ~ VaNessa Sikes Young
Elisa S. Harney ~ Coretta E. Pitters
Victory Lowe ~ Betty Bridges
Angier S. Johnson ~ LaToya S. Bell ~ Choona Lang
Stephanie L. Provitt ~ Keisha D. Thomas
Cassandra Wheeler ~ Kathy T. McFadden

Edited, Compiled, Forward by
W. R. Coleman

only two PA programs in Alabama at the time, one of which was my *alma mater*, USA, I only applied to USA in 2006. I was granted an interview and was accepted into the program in 2007. And, as the old saying goes, the rest is history.

By no means was this an easy task for me in that my PA program was a very long, hard, and grueling 27 months, especially since I was married and had 2 young children: one in college and one in middle school. But, with the help of my Lord and Savior, my husband, parents, and siblings, WE made it through, graduating in 2009. My greatest motivation to succeed is my family. They've always been in my corner.

While attending PA school, sacrifices were made in that I was unable to work for those 27 months of the program. Because the program was so grueling and time consuming, my parents allowed my youngest, my son, to stay with them until I finished the program. Not only did I sacrifice, but my husband sacrificed as well. After I was accepted into the PA program, I resigned from my nursing job, which meant we went from a two-income family to a one-income family, with my husband being the sole provider. That was a long, hard, 27 months. But God!!!

This path challenged me mentally, physically, and spiritually, but by the grace & mercy of God, I was able to remain committed and determined to reach that goal. Something inside me refused to let me settle. It was not easy, but it has certainly been worth it. I am currently employed at Physicians Care of Thomasville with Dr. Huey Kidd. I've been with Dr. Kidd for almost 7 years and counting. My job is very fulfilling for me as well as for my patients. I get to do every day what I've always wanted to do, help and minister to people physically, mentally, and spiritually. To God be the Glory!

Wait! That's not the end of my story . . . for a while now, I've had a desire to advance my career to another level. Completing the PA program was indeed an accomplishment, but I just felt like there was something else, something more, something greater for me. So about seven months ago, I enrolled as a student at the University of Lynchburg to pursue my PhD!

Teaching has always been in my spirit, and God has opened the door for me to manifest it. I just believe that because I didn't settle, He's giving me the desires of my heart. If you're reading this and there's a dream in your heart, I encourage you to go for it! Seek His will, let Him guide you, and give Him the glory in advance. You can do it! I'm not telling you what I've heard. I'm telling you what I know! Don't settle. Go for it!

Victoria is happily married to Dale T. Howard, with two children, Adrian and Melchizedek. Her work as a PA in Thomasville is a tremendous blessing to her community. She thankfully anticipates graduation and receiving her Doctor of Medical Science (DMSc) degree from University of Lynchburg in May.

Just Breathe . . . God is Always in Control

SHABRA COLEMAN-GOODMAN

I don't know what made that day different from the other days. I don't know why, that day, of all days, I found that overwhelming Herculean strength and courage. Even now, nearly four years later, I wonder if that strength would have been enough. If he had come home while I was desperately trying to fit ten years of my life into the back of my black Impala. If he had called to say he was on the way home. If the 16x20 wedding picture hanging on the wall, crooked from the last door slamming, had caught my eye. Would I have changed my mind, or would I have kept going? Would I still have run for my life? But he didn't come home. He didn't call home. And that crooked wedding picture blended so well into the sad and melancholy walls that I didn't even notice it. On that day, September 9, 2010 at 9:58 a.m., I left behind what started out as a fairytale marriage but had somehow become volatile.

I can remember that drive to my parent's house. I remember how it felt like I couldn't breathe. I was suffocating from the weight of the decision I had just made. With every breathe came another question. Breathe. "Am I doing the right thing?" "Breathe." "What else could I have done?" "Breathe." "What would I do with the rest of my life? "Breathe." That's what I told myself over and over again. "Breathe, Shabra, breathe!" "Keep breathing and keep driving......breathe."

I had to keep reminding myself to breathe over the next several months. Eventually, like a newborn baby, I began to breathe on my own, without the guided assistance of my heart. Everything was looking okay but I still did not know what I would do with the rest of my life. Until I saw a commercial on television that would change my life.

An Art Institute commercial came on, and just like that, I had my answer. I called the school in Atlanta, Georgia and made an appointment to go and visit. Three months later, I moved to Atlanta to start the rest of my life.

The next year of my life was one of the hardest years I had ever experienced. I was alone in a city full of people. I had left everything and everyone I knew and loved to come to a city where I knew and loved no one. For the first couple months, I stayed in an apartment provided by the school. The school had so graciously informed me that they would provide an apartment for me. The tiny 3-bedroom apartment would also have five other students in it as well.

I had encountered some issues during my stay there. Not to mention, I was much older than the teens that were rooming with me. I went to the housing department, the dean, the president and complained about the housing conditions. They promised by the next semester they would have finished renovation on another apartment building and we would be spread out. I was excited for the next semester only to find out that because of a "glitch" in the system, my name was no longer on the housing list. I was on my own for a place to stay. Coincidence?

I had just started a job as a line cook at an Italian restaurant called Gianni's at Lake Lanier Resorts, in Gainesville, (about 1 hour from Atlanta). It was the middle of the summer by now, hot and muggy in Georgia. The little money that I made covered my gas back and forth to work, school supplies and uniforms. I could not afford an apartment, so I slept in my car for a few months: 5am school…2pm work….11pm find a safe place to park and sleep.

That was my life. I tried to just keep breathing normal, as if life had not just knocked be flat on my behind. I fought off panic attacks every time I thought about the reality of my situation. Had I done the wrong thing by coming here? Did I move too fast? I remember one night, after work, I was sitting in the parking lot.

Too exhausted mentally and physically to drive to find a parking lot, I was praying to God to make it clear to me what to do next when I looked down and saw my legs and ankles so swollen and discolored from sitting in the car and working continuously. The sight of them scared me so bad that I jumped out of the car and began to walk as fast as I could away from it. I walked and cried and prayed and pleaded to God for help.

By the time I got to the shore's edge, I was so exhausted that I stretched out on the shore and went to sleep. The sun shining brightly into my eyes woke me up. The bottom of my cook pants, my feet, shoes and socks were soaking wet from the water splashing up on me during the night. I sat up and began to take off my soaked shoes and socks only to see my ankles were nowhere near as swollen as they looked the night before.

Had my view of my swollen ankles and legs the night before been a figment of my imagination or had God allowed the waters to wash away the pain and swelling so I could go on a little further? I chose to believe the later.... looked up at the sky and said, Thank you God for my answer. *I understand, You are still in control.*

From time to time, I still find myself having to remind myself to breathe. But this time, it's not because I'm feeling the heavy weight of the decisions I made. It's because I'm breathless from the possibilities before me. "Breathe." I keep telling myself. *"Breathe. God is still in control!"*

Shabra currently lives in Montgomery, Alabama, and has worked in hospital nutrition since her arrival here. She & her wonderfully supportive husband, Maceo Goodman, are professional chefs & entrepreneurs who own Nostalgia Smokehouse & Catering. They perfectly balance one another and look forward to all that God has planned for them.

The Miracle After the Storm

MONICA SARGENT

I heard someone say once that storms don't always come to cause "destruction" but sometimes come to clear a path. Wow! This couldn't have been truer and exactly what I needed during my storms; however, this revelation came after the storm.

As we travel this road of life, we take many turns, shortcuts, detours, and U-turns not realizing that with each trip, there is something to be learned, left behind, abandoned, gained, forgiven. I can't say exactly when the storm arrived but I'm sure there were signs, "newsflashes", and "alerts" I missed or chose to ignore. But God!

Many times, we see ourselves through the eyes of others: their expectations, their perceptions, their thoughts of us. So much so that we begin to take on the character of those ideas or labels people have thought about or placed on us. I'd like to believe after salvation all those thoughts and labels are washed away by the blood of Jesus and, in a sense, they really are. We sometimes reach and grab those thoughts and labels before they can be completely washed away and wrap them around us again as if we are naked without them.

Now this is nothing that I've been told, nor have I read about, I am speaking from experience. You may be reading this and thinking to yourself, "Well, I know who I am and who God has created me to be." If that's true and you really know who you are, that is awesome, and I praise God for your revelation!

But I write to encourage those who still may be struggling with embracing God's love for them. Yes, as messed up as we are, God loves us. He proved His love for us by sending His only begotten Son, Jesus, to die for our sins. But Jesus' death released so much more. *"But God commendeth his love toward us, in that while we were yet sinners, Christ died for us"* (Romans 5:8 KJV). The Amplified Bible states it like this, *"But God shows and clearly proves His [own] love for us by the fact that while we were still sinners, Christ (the Messiah, the Anointed One) died for us."*(Romans 5:8 NKJV) Wow! If God loved us that much before salvation, how much more can He love us after salvation - still with our issues and hang-ups. Oh, the wonderful grace of Jesus!

It took me understanding the grace of God to understand the purpose of my storms, and it took me understanding the purpose of my storms to understand the grace of God. I recall driving home one day after a "quick" storm passed through our area. It seemed like so much rain fell in a matter of minutes. The Holy Spirit reminded me of Isaiah 55:10-11. *"For as the rain comes down, and the snow from heaven, and do not return there, but water the earth, and make it bring forth and bud, that it may give seed to the sower and bread to the eater, so shall My word be that goes forth out of My mouth; it shall not return to Me void, but it shall accomplish what I please, and it shall prosper in the thing for which I sent it"* (NKJV).

What the Holy Spirit was telling me was there is a purpose for every rain drop that falls to the earth. The same principle applies to our lives. There is purpose for every drop of rain that falls in our lives, every storm, every bad day, and every good day. I'll never forget the day God pushed me into a place where I had no other choice than to trust Him.

I couldn't go to this person or that person for the solution, the answer, the resolution. The day/days when it seemed like God shut everyone's mouth around me so that my only choice was to seek Him, listen for His voice, and TRUST. Trust that God had me in a place of "isolation" for my good. I had become so dependent on people to tell me I was "going in the right direction" that "I was doing the right things" until I no longer went to God for direction but sought after the approval of people.

Until that day God allowed the Holy Spirit to show me the essence of my heart. *Essence: the nature or quality of something.* Pain, bitterness, unforgiveness, fear, pride, many unhealthy attachments, and dwindling faith was what occupied my heart. How was there room for anything else? At that moment I had to make a choice, allow God to clean me up or keep on rockin' like everything was alllll good. So I chose to get back on the potter's wheel and with that choice, my life seemed to crumble.

Oh, how I screamed, cried, prayed, begged God to clean me up, get rid of all the filth the Holy Spirit had shown me. But to be honest, I wanted the "quick deliverance" so no one would notice I "needed deliverance." Silly me! God always knows and He has equipped some to see. But deliverance didn't come quick, God didn't pull me out of the "storm" just because I failed to bring a raincoat or an umbrella.

I had to ride this storm out. Like a ship being ripped from the dock, God's Word began ripping away those unhealthy attachments. Those people, things, thoughts that had become my "crutch". His Word, the Holy Spirit, and His awesome presence began exposing the places where unforgiveness, bitterness, fear, and pride originated; painful relationships, the need to feel appreciated or important, the fear of not being good enough.

Everything the Holy Spirit exposed, I had to either carry to Jesus or hold on to it and remain in bondage. I had no time to go backwards because God had taken all my "go to" options away . . . I HAD TO TRUST, God was my only hope.

Guess what, I had people, who actually "saw" me before I saw myself, praying for me and I had no idea. You do too!! When I decided that "hiding" my condition was no longer an option, I found that I wasn't the only one! Jesus explained those who are well don't need a physician, but those who are sick do (Matthew 9:12). I was spiritually sick and in desperate need of help. See, the enemy's desire is for us to view our storms, the things we go through in life, as being negative and his plot is to make us feel as if "we are the only ones" experiencing this or that. Furthermore, the enemy desires to make us believe God does not or could not love us.

That is so far from the truth. John 8:32 says "and you shall know the truth and the truth shall make you free" (NIV). The truth is "For God so loved the world that He gave His only begotten Son, that whoever believes in Him should not perish but have everlasting life." Now tell me that's not love!

I had to remember Romans 8:28, *"And we know that all things work together for good to those who love God, to those who are the called according to His purpose"* (NKJV). Every word that God spoke before the storm, during the storm, after the storm: it has, or it will accomplish just what He purposed it to. It's not going to return unto Him void but it's going to accomplish that which He pleases and prosper in the thing whereto He sent it. Now that's something to shout about!

My pastor, Rev. Ricky Chambers, Sr., said, "Our storms don't come to take us out, they come to take us in!" They come to take us into the presence of God, into the secret place where we begin to learn more about who He (God Almighty, Jehovah) is and how desperately we need God the Father, His Son Jesus our Savior, and the Holy Spirit our Helper.

There are some trees that need to be knocked down in our lives in order to allow the S-O-N to shine through. These trees only a storm can uproot! Trees of pride, self-righteousness, unbelief, unforgiveness, past hurts and offenses, and the list goes on. God allows storms to come to be sure those trees are moved out of the way so that the Son can heal and replenish us with His love. Remember, Jesus' death and resurrection gave us access to so much. *"But He was wounded for our transgressions, He was bruised for our iniquities; the chastisement of our peace was upon Him, and by His stripes we are healed"* (Isaiah 53:5 NKJV).

We may not even recognize some of the things that can and will hinder our walk with Christ and hinder us from experiencing an intimate relationship with Jesus which we cannot afford to live without. I recall the instance in which Jesus and the disciples were *"going to the other side"* and *"there arose a great storm"* (Mark 4:35-41 NIV). This storm was rough! So much so that the disciples began to panic and question whether Jesus cared if they perished or not. In the middle of the storm the disciples forgot to take full advantage of the relationship they had or should have had with Him. Jesus simply rebuked the wind and said to the sea, *"Peace be still."*

I can relate to the disciples. I've been there. Going through storms caused by life and my choices and panicking although I claimed to be "trusting God" and all those other clichés we use! Crying out to Jesus to "get me out," "rescue me," "help me," and completely missing the purpose of the storm. The purpose of the storm was to increase my faith, stimulate a greater dependency on God, and to grow me up! Lord, the lost time I wasted trying to get out or be rescued, and the lessons I missed by not recognizing the purpose of the storms.

I want to encourage you so that whenever you find yourself in a storm, though it may seem as if it is going to take you out, hang on. It has a purpose. The Bible teaches us to *"give thanks IN everything for this is the will of God in Christ Jesus concerning us"* (I Thessalonians 5:18 NKJV). Keep pushing, keep pressing, and don't give up! You may be in a storm now and will probably go through more storms throughout this journey called life, but don't fret. I am a living witness there is a miracle after the storm!

Am I saying I have it all together now? NOT AT ALL!!! But now I know to run to Jesus with my issues, and not from Him. I am continually learning to buckle up and embrace the storms of life because they will come. And they always have purpose.

Will you allow me to pray for you?

*God, I thank You for the person reading this article at this moment.
I praise You that in Your infinite wisdom, You poured into me that
I may pour out to Your people to encourage when encouragement
is needed the most. I bless You because You are Elohim. You can
create something beautiful and extraordinary from of our lives.
Today, we grant You permission to do so in the Name of Jesus!*

*Thank You that strength is coming to the reader right now in the
Name of Jesus. They are receiving strength to endure the storm, strength*

to focus on You because we understand that our help comes from You (Psalm 121:1-2 NIV). You are a present help in time of trouble (Psalm 46:1 NIV). God, thank You for this opportunity to share what You've taught me. I am truly humbled by this opportunity.

God, for the reader who does not know Jesus as their personal Savior, I ask that You accept them into Your family just as You've accepted me. For You told us in Your word that "**if we confess with our mouth the Lord Jesus and believe in our heart that God has raised Him from the dead, we shall be saved. For with the heart one believes unto righteousness, and with the mouth confession is made unto salvation**" *(Romans 10:9-10 NKJV. May their lives be a manifestation of Your Glory!! In Jesus' Name, Amen.*

Monica serves as a worship leader at her church, New Vision Baptist Church, in Waynesboro. Having earned her bachelor's degree in Social Work from Mississippi State University, she is also a social worker who is blessed to help create families through adoption. In addition to her relationship with Jesus Christ, her greatest joys are her family which includes her husband, Terence, and her children Ta'Keecia and Sekeedrick, her parents, sisters, nieces & nephews, and her New Vision Church family.

Learning to Trust So That I May Teach

Mamie C. Thompson

First and foremost. I need to say, "Thank You God!" No matter what I've been through, no matter where I've been to, no matter the outcome, I NEED to say, "Thank You God!"

Just sitting here now as I've done so many times, I think back to what my life has truly become thus far. I've always believed that God does everything for me, He does not ever leave me, He's always the same. He's the same today, yesterday and forever. I've always believed God takes care of me and takes me to places where I am supposed to be according to His will. I'm going to tell you a little about my journey and what my report looks like.

After high school, in 1984, I entered college. My goal was to be a teacher. I really liked college, but I wasn't as dedicated as I should have been. To me, it was all about being away from home, on my own, not realizing that the opportunity given to me was one that others would have been so very grateful if given the chance. Well, college life came to an end. I was forced to get a job to help with home, myself, and my daughter. My mother and father were a big support in helping to raise my daughter while I was out "finding myself".

Then, I found a job in retail. I really liked being out there among people, working in the stores, helping, doing all sorts of different and exciting things. And, I was so good at it. I got content and said to myself, "I've finally found something I'm good at!". So, I thought I would continue and go forward with no worries. But life happens, right? I found a man that I fell in live with or I thought I knew what love was, and we got married, had two more children and it all began. My life, I thought, God had given me the perfect husband, the perfect job, the perfect family, the peace I was looking for and felt I needed in my life. But things happened that should have never happened, and my marriage fell apart. We divorced and my life as I knew it was over.

I began to ask God, "WHY"? Why did you do this to me?? I tried to be a good wife, a good mother, a good person, why did you let this happen to me? At that time, I questioned my own faith. I knew in my heart that God had done what He thought was best for my life at that time. It took a while, but I knew. He had other plans for me. It took me a while to see and I begged God to forgive me for not trusting Him. He did and I know He did. I wrote so many times to Him and prayed so much for God to show me what I needed to do. To show me what His plan was for me.

God gave me another opportunity in 2005. I had then moved on to another retail company, one of the biggest companies in the world, and I thought I had hit the jackpot. I moved my way up to store manager and managed three stores during my 14 years with the company. So, I thanked God and said this is where my life is supposed to be. I became content and I always kept in the back of my mind, I wish I had just finished college when I was given the opportunity.

So, while I was managing, I began taking online classes. Everything was going well, I met a wonderful man that became my husband. I prayed to God that if it was His will for me to marry again, please let him be a Godly man. Let him be the man that He has for me. God sent me the very best husband. I know He was hand-picked and waiting for me, he's my life and I thank God for him.

As I continued my career in retail and I had married the man I knew I would spend the rest of my life with, things began to happen with my job. People were in place to hurt and destroy everything I had built in my career. I lost my job and I was so devastated. I was truly hurt. But GOD, but GOD, but GOD!! I want you to know that I did not question God about this. My faith is so heavy and real that I knew God had other plans for me. I thought this was what I was to do, but God had other plans. I can truly tell you if I didn't know that, I would have treated Him the same way I did when my first marriage fell apart.

That was the old me, this is the new me. I believe in Him, I trust Him with all my heart. God had put in my life at this time a supportive and loving husband, a non-judgmental family and a host of true friends to help me through this trying time. He already knew this was going to happen, so I dared not to question Him. My Pastor helped me also to remember that God never puts more on us than we can bear, through all trials and tribulations, we must count it all joy. He has his reasons when we go through but it's how we handle those trials that will make us strong if we endure to the end. No matter what, count it all joy!

Today, God has given me another job that I truly love, still in retail and its good. He has shown me that what I wanted to accomplish in 1984 is still available if I want it and trust that He will provide the way. I applied for college in 2018 to go back and finish my degree so I can become a teacher and open my own daycare. I prayed to God that if this is my path, please provide the way.

The quarter came, I'd gotten all the application papers in and financial aid, then waiting on an answer. The letter came and, I was so excited. I opened and read, *"Dear Mamie, we regret to inform you that you have been denied financial aid for the fall semester."* My mind went into a mode of disbelief. I said well maybe God is not ready for me to do this yet. But He put it on my husband's heart and provided the way to pay for the semester. I knew then, God is still in charge! I finished the semester on the President's List! Now going into the Spring semester, God has taken care of all my financial needs with a Pell Grant. *Ain't God good?* Do you know how many times I've thanked Him and continually thank Him? I, at 52 years old, am going back to school to finish what God had for me in the beginning.

As I stated at the beginning, I can only say "Thank You God!" I Thank you for everything, my ups, my downs, my good times, my bad times, even when I didn't thank you when I should have, you kept on giving and loving me. Sometimes I didn't deserve your love, but you kept right on and for this I say, Thank You.

My report is that God does what He says He will do, and He does it repeatedly just as He has done and continues to do in my life. He's given me that husband, that family, that life that I'm supposed to have according to His will.

Mamie is happily married to Horace Thompson and is blessed to have 3 awesome children – Courtney, Shaquia, Isaiah – and 8 sweet grands. She's active at New Prospect Missionary Baptist Church in Nettleton, Mississippi, where she serves as Church Clerk, sings in the choir, serves on the missionary board, and works with the youth of the church to help them understand how much God loves them. Currently an operations manager with Office Depot Company, Mamie is also pursuing her degree in Childhood Education at Itawamba Community College. She looks forward to opening a childcare center upon completion of her degree.

If He Did It for Me . . .

FELICIA REED-TAYLOR

God knew one day I would need the grip of His mercy to hold me together, and 2005 was the appointed time. I was in my darkest hour, but God was about to make it my finest time. I began to cry out to God for help because I had been living two lives far too long. I was secretly sinning and openly serving God . . . or so I thought. Then God in His infinite ways exposed all the wrong in me so that He could reveal what was right in me. This is my "mess turned message," so let me tell you how God did it for me.

Gambling addict, thief, liar, cheater and so much more that was contrary to who God designed me to be & who He knew I was. But one day I heard the voice of the Lord say to me, *I still purposed you for greatness and you must fulfill the plan that I have for your life* (Jeremiah 29:11 NIV). God loved me so much that even in the middle of my mess, He gave me a way of escape. He took me to a place where I had to undergo a serious period of self-inventory. God reminded me during that very painful time that He sent His son to the cross to die for my sins. But I had to repent and turn away from the lifestyle that was killing me. It was the power in the blood of Jesus' that enabled me to do so.

While I was still trying to claw my way out of sin, the word of God strengthened my spirit as I recalled that *if any man be in Christ, he is a new creature* (II Corinthians 5:17 NIV). Old things, old sins, old ways, old failures had to pass away, and everything had to become new in my life. I was after all born again, and I knew Him to be *Jehovah-Jira*, the Lord who provides, and *Jehovah-Rapha*, the Lord God who heals. In order to be completely delivered, I had to allow Him to become *Jehovah-Shalom*, my God of peace.

If I was going to do what God had called me to do, I would have to let some things go. Indeed, even let some people go. Everyone would not understand where God was taking me. Even I didn't fully understand but I knew I could not stay in sin. I had to let go and let God take total control of my life and take me the way in which He knew would be best.

My mugshot was on every media outlet in town as a fugitive, but I didn't know and wasn't running from the law. I was being investigated for forgery (10 counts) and theft of property I due to my addiction to gambling. Never thought that all the additional checks I wrote to myself from my employer would be the paper trail that would have me arrested in the natural as well as in the spirit. I learned quickly that God's *thoughts were not my thoughts neither were His ways my way*s. I believe now that I **had to** be exposed in this manner.

I found myself standing before the judge looking at 2–22 years in prison on each of the 11 felony counts pending against me. I could literally hear my heart beats as I stood for sentencing and the judge said, "***Young lady, I see some good in you, so I am not going to send you to prison***." Instead he sentenced me to a program called pre-trial diversion which was run by the local District Attorney's office. I looked at my lawyer, looked back at my family, told God thank you and said, "***Now you order my steps God***."

Without the grace of God, the headlines would have read "*Felicia Reed-Taylor has been found guilty of theft of property I and ten counts of forgery.*" God's report said, "guilty but forgiven." By the grace of God: that was the only way I received another chance to get it right with God. I had a long road ahead of me, but I did the work necessary to complete the pre-trial diversion program. God put me in a group that would be known as Team Redeemed. My counselor was a Godly woman who took a vested interest in my walk with God and worked with me above and beyond her duties.

A dear loved one who was a crack addict for 25 years became my prayer partner and confidant throughout my process. He was the one God used to pour into my life the word of God and show me true Agape. About 5 years later (the number of grace), God showed Himself mighty in my life. That same loved one told me I would go on television and host a Christian show (local TBN), it happened. He told me the very people that talked about and laughed at me would ask for forgiveness. True to his prophetic utterance, that happened. He told me I would go into ministry and speak God's word to people who were hurting and looking for hope. That happened too. I thank God that I accepted my call-in ministry in 2009 and have been an ordained Minister since 2013.

My closing message to you: purpose leads you to destiny – even when your actions & decisions threaten to derail that destiny - and destiny leads you to God who will reveal His plan for your life. Take it from a sister who knows. If He did it for me, He can do it for you and use you for such a time as this.

Felicia Reed Taylor is the wife of Robert Taylor and mother to one daughter, Kayla Cierra Taylor. She is a 1994 graduate of Alabama State University with a BA degree in Communications - Radio/TV Broadcasting. Taylor was the host of Joy In Our Town, a community and public affairs show on the local Trinity Broadcast Network (TBN). She is currently employed with Alabama State University in the Division of Continuing Education as a Program Assistant. In her spare time, she enjoys mentoring  *women in transition from past challenges in life and assisting them in reaching their full potential. She lives by her favorite scripture, Jeremiah 29:11.*

Living Well . . . On Purpose

CHOONA LANG

Life is filled with many challenges and distractions that tend to block our view of the important things in life. God did not promise us sunshine every day but he did promise us that our storms would not last always. Therefore, when the storms of life come we must trust God's plan to work everything out for our good. For we walk by faith and not by sight. In the mist of what seems like endless confusion, crime, budget shortfalls, hunger, sickness, poor leadership, and homelessness, we must remember that through it all; God is still in control. Even when we can't physically see our way through, God has a way of sending messages our way to let you know that the **Son will** shine again.

Just think about the children of Israel wilderness experience. In a dark place in their life out of nowhere God provided manna and quails for physical nourishment, clouds in the day to guide their path, without extreme heat from sun. When we stop and really meditate on the goodness of God he always supplies our needs. We waste too much of our precious time trying to figure things out when God has already worked them out. Just step back, take a deep breath, and relax because God knows all about it and in his timing he will make your path clear.

Don't allow life' temporary moments of distractions prevent you from receiving the greater blessing on the other side of the storm. Don't allow life distractions to stop you from living well daily and from growing in God' anointing. Don't give in to the negative verbal or written attacks to make you feel less than the wonderful person God made you to be. Reject the voices in your mind that are dragging your pass back in front of your face. Let those voices know that you are not your past, you are a unique child of God designed to positively impact the body of Christ grow in your anointing.

There are no real magical steps to making healthy life choices and growing in your anointing, but the key is consistency. Consistent prayer and strengthen your faith walk and fellowship with Christ so that you can draw from the living well during the time of your earthly draught. Consistent rest so our thought process can be clear. Consistent water to maintain proper hydration which is needed to enhance organ functions (spiritual water- Anointing growth). Consistent healthy food choices in proper portions, for your body, to maintain the daily energy needed to live well. This life formula positions you in a right state of mind to receive your daily heavenly instructions.

Nurture your Anointing includes:

1. Plan to live well. The best course of action tends to begin with a well-designed plan. Jeremiah 29:11 *11 For I know the plans I have for you," declares the LORD, "PLANS TO PROSPER YOU AND NOT TO HARM YOU, PLANS TO GIVE YOU HOPE AND A FUTURE.* (NIV)
2. Activate the Plan. Living by Faith is an action word. *Hebrew 11:1 Now faith is confidence in what we hope for and assurance about what we do not see. (NIV)*
3. Evaluate the Plan- 2 Peter: 12-13 Therefore, I will always remind you about these things—even though you already know them and are standing firm in the truth you have been taught. And it is only right that I should keep on reminding you as long as I live. (NLT)
4. Modify the Plan as needed- Ephesians 3:20-21 **20 Now to him who is able to do immeasurably more than all we ask or imagine, according to his power that is at work within us, 21 to him be glory in the church and in Christ Jesus throughout all generations, forever and ever! Amen. (NIV)**

As women of God we must be lifelong learners always willing and open to go deeper with/in God's words. This cycle should be repeated until we have reached our eternal destination. ***Live Well Everyday through Jesus Christ as we grow in his anointing should be a lifestyle. God Bless you all as you intentionally listen for our Heavenly father' daily instructions to live well, which will grow our anointing. Never lose sight of the fact that it is his power that we stand on and not our self-will.***

Choona is a native of Montgomery. Daughter of Mr. Willie and Theresa Jones, she is married to Cornelius Lang and the mother of two children, Myia, son-in-law, Jatori Graves and son Marcus. Choona has four living biologic sisters and one sister in heaven. She completed the Doctoral of Health Education Program in the fall of 2016. She is employed with the Alabama Department of Public Health as the Home Care Division Director. She is an active member of Mt. Gillard Baptist Church where she is Director of Christian Education, Health & Wellness and Social Services Ministry.

Releasing the Prophetic in Your Life

VaNessa Sykes-Young

First a little bit about me: I reside in Sheffield Village, a small town west of Cleveland, Ohio. For the last eight years I have had the great pleasure of co-pastoring Point of Grace Ministries with my husband of 16 years, and we are the proud parents of two young men (Zion, 15 and Avery, 13). Before we received our call to lead God's people, we were at separate ministries. We now know why God didn't have one of us join the other. He had His own plan to bring us together. Revelation came through obedience and not listening to others who said the wife must follow her husband. Many times, when people presented that unwarranted opinion, my husband's response would simply be, *"God didn't tell me that."*

Neither I nor my husband is a "preacher's kid" nor did we come from the lineage of prophets. God gave me visions and spoke to me in such ways that I had no personal knowledge of anyone experiencing their call in this manner. I might also mention that I was reared in a predominately white community in which I was one of two students in the graduating class!

During my journey in ministry, I have learned the value of prophetic release and want to share some insight with you in hopes that it will bless you. There are three groups of believers I have encountered. The first group believes that prophets are not for today. The second group believes prophets are fake and want money. The third are open minded but just have never had the opportunity to meet a prophet. Well I am one that you are meeting in writing who will address all three.

Group #1 - Scriptures declares in Joel 2:28 & Acts 2:17 *"In the last days, God says, I will pour out my Spirit on all people. Your sons and your daughters will prophesy, your young men will see visions, and your old men will dream dreams."* (NIV) I don't believe this has to do with age but the believer's maturity level in God. Both of these Scriptural passages actually pertain to today.

Group #2 – In II Peter 2:1, the Word tells us *"But there were also fake prophets among the people, just as there will be false teachers among you."(NIV)* This scripture reveals that many will be led astray because they did not heed the words of the prophets. Prophets have been given the task of speaking the heart of God. The Bible makes it clear you shall know a tree by the fruit it bears. True prophets of God will bring correction, direction & comfort, without leading the people to them – the prophets - but turning the hearts of man back to the Father.

Group #3 - Revelation 2:29 exhorts *"whoever has ears, let them hear what the Spirit says to the churches."* (NKJV) The heart needs to be receptive. Prophecy is revelation from God. As His children, we do not have the right nor authority to tell God how to speak to us. Being the mother of two, sometimes my boys don't appreciate my tone or timing of our conversations I initiate, but I am still their parent. I don't give them the option of how or when I choose to communicate with them! I believe this is the same perspective our Heavenly Father has toward us.

My call experience came through an open vision. Open visions occur when the recipient is wide awake. My first experience with an open vision occurred while worshiping at church, my hands were lifted in the air the Lord rolled what I can only describe as a scroll in front of me. Everything was so detailed that I knew exactly where it was taking place. It was the hall where my wedding reception was held eight years prior. I was standing behind a podium preaching the Gospel when God said, *"I called you to feed my sheep."*

I received guidance through prophetic revelations from God. I had no blueprints to follow. There were no A, B, C's or 1, 2,3's. My directions, whether we are talking about what building to purchase, to how to design the building, to starting a prophetic school were birthed out of God revealing through visions or prophetic releases when it was only Him and I. He would be so detailed that even when the architect tried to encourage me to change the layout of our edifice, the Lord told me to build like Solomon and He showed me every placement necessary for His Glory to be in the house. I asked God one time why I didn't have a mentor at the time to help me to understand the language of God. His response was *"the Holy Spirit will teach you, man will not get the glory for what I do in and through you."*(John 16:13 NIV)

Webster's defines releasing as *allowing (something) to move or act, or flow freely.* Point of Grace Ministries was birthed out of the free-flowing move of God. I was opposed more than applauded by the very ones that were supposed to nurture and care for me. I could not and would not allow a hurt to hinder a call. Had I not responded to a prophetic vision which really is the way God chose to speak to me, the remnant of believers that were getting wounded along with me Sunday after Sunday would not have found rest for their weary souls.

Their spirits show 'nuff was willing but their flesh was getting weak! My life would not be as fulfilling as it is, and I must admit, challenging at times without the prophetic call on my life. I now train and equip young prophets on how to hear God and tune out other voices. I believe there are many Samuels to train prophets and Nehemiahs to rebuild torn down walls, but it will only take place when they surrender to the prophetic release in their lives.

VaNessa is a woman of God & leader who loves her family to life. Being a blessing to God's people is at the heart of the ministry she provides as a modern-day prophetess. Unapologetic about the call that God has on her life, she celebrates every moment and endeavors to help others do the same.

God Turned it All the Way Around

Elisa Sanders Harney

By definition, "turn" means that something changes in its nature, state or form. Each time I reflect on all the "turning" that I've experienced in my life, I always come back to one, in particular: When God turned my MESS into a MIRACLE. Webster defines a "mess" as a dirty or untidy state of things; it's also defined as a situation or state of affairs that is confused or full of difficulties. That was certainly my life at one point. I found myself in a constant state of either MAKING a mess…or BEING a mess. When we use the word "mess," it's usually in reference to something that is dirty, disorganized or in disarray. Our hair, our office, our relationships. It's rarely used to depict something good or positive. Why? Because my MESS is a direct reflection of ME. And so, we begin a guilt-ridden disassociation from our MESS. I took it a step further and decided that M.E.S.S. was **M**y **E**mbarrassing **S**hameful **S**ituation. May I ask you a question? Have you ever dealt with a MESS in your own life? If the answer is yes, then keep reading.

I didn't want people to know about My Embarrassing Shameful Situation. As a matter of fact, let's put an "s" on situation. There were most certainly more than one. Pregnancy out of wedlock? MESS. College dropout? MESS. Failed marriage? MESS. Loss of job? MESS. Single parent of 3? MESS. I could go on, but I think you get the picture. So, what do you do when you're in a mess? Well, let's look at it in the natural. If our house is in a mess, the last thing we want is for someone to come over for dinner. Why? Because it exposes the fact that we've been neglectful about our priorities and responsibilities with no accountability. Whew! That was a hard but necessary pill for me to swallow. I live by a simple yet direct motto:

You can't FIX what you won't FACE. My life was a mess and this time the uninvited guest was God. I didn't want HIM coming over for dinner when my house was dirty, disorganized and in disarray. I gave no thought of His desire or ability to turn my situation around. I was too busy being overwhelmed, oppressed and ostracized. This is the place where we make our first mistake. When we realize that we've either made a mess or become a mess, the first thing we opt to do is hide, deny, blame or justify. Sound familiar? If you can't say "Amen" at least say "Ouch." We think that if we hide it, it will cease to exist. If we deny it, we can make everyone else look crazy. If we shift blame, we can become the victim. And if there's a reasonable cause, we're justified…and that's acceptable. My Embarrassing Shameful Situation.

God gave me an amazing revelation about His divine ability to "turn" even in My Embarrassing Shameful Situation (MESS) that I'd like to share with you. I once read an article in an apartment therapy magazine that listed 5 reasons why your place is in a mess. The more I read, the clearer I became about myself.

1. **You pile paper (mail, books, coupons, magazines).** *They're sprinkled in every room — on top of dressers, in bags, stuffed in drawers, sitting on tables collecting dust. What do all of these types of paper have in common? They all hold information. And, guess what? Most of that information is out of date. But we keep it. Why? Because we might want to go back and **remember** something. We need to be **reminded** of an event. We want to keep a **record** of an occurrence. We never get to the point of purging. We become hoarders. We also do this electronically. Should I even ask when was the last time you purged your emails? And let's not forget our cellphones. Old text messages. Screenshots. Photos from 3 years ago. Things that we could back up to the cloud or archive online. It makes it next to impossible to add or upgrade new apps, record videos or take any additional photos. You*

can't download anything NEW because you have insufficient storage. We keep trying to operate on a limited space capacity. It's the same emotionally. We keep records, reminders and remembrances of faults, failures and foolery. People that hurt, abandoned, betrayed or rejected us. Times when we were filled with grief, shame and resentment. We fail to understand that we can archive the memories and free the space. Instead, we hoard grudges, fear, superficial associations, unforgiveness, unhealthy "soul ties" and life leeches and our lives stay in a mess.

2. **You don't put things back where they belong.** *My mom used to have a quote posted in our hallway when I was younger that said, "A place for everything and everything in its place." The problem is that we rarely do that. We start on one task, get interrupted or sidetracked, then go to the next without first putting up what we were initially working on. Why? Simple: we're certain that we'll get back to it as some point. I'm bad at it. "Leave it right there, I'm going to finish it in a minute." Days will go by and I'll have completely forgotten about it. That is, until I'm looking for something that I left right along with my abandoned project. Isn't that what we do in life? We have displaced emotions from our past that don't belong in the place where we are now, but we keep wanting to "get back to it" at some point. People have mistreated us, rejected us, betrayed us and left us. Years have passed yet we're still carrying those feelings right up into our adult life. Now we're transferring those feelings of suspicion, distrust and insecurity unto people that never did anything to you. Why? Because you didn't put those emotions back where they belong. A MESS. Guess what? You can't GROW without letting GO.*

3. **You don't have a solution for worn/dirty/used clothes.** *This is one of the most common culprits of a messy space. It's hard to break a habit of leaving clothes where they are when you take them off. Who hasn't ever hung a shirt or pair of pants that weren't "really" dirty over the arm of a chair. What about that outfit that doesn't really fit, is no longer your style or has seen better days? Even worse, that shirt or pair of jeans with the spot that refuses to come out? Why do we keep things around? No solution for things that are worn, dirty and used up. It's what we do relationally as well. We're holding on to superficial associations and toxic relationships that cause our bodies to*

feel used, our minds to feel dirty and our emotions to feel worn out. We keep things past its expiration date. We can smell that it's spoiled. We can see where it's beginning to rot. We understand that ingesting its toxicity will make us sick to our stomach and yet we keep retreating to it like a fly to a garbage can. Was that it bit much? Good. That's why it's called MESS. My Embarrassing Shameful Situation.

4. **You think you've cleaned more recently than you have.** *Memory can be a liar. Deceptive. You think you mopped a few days ago and realize that it was really the week before last. You could've sworn you just did the laundry the other day when in actuality it was the other week. Things start piling up little by little. Until one day we look up and there are piles of laundry, dishes, and dust that have been accumulating right under our nose. That's exactly what happens with us. We say we're over something when the truth is that we're still angry. We think we've gotten past it when we're bitter. Still grappling with rejection. Still processing the abandonment. Still grieving. Still hurting. Still bleeding. Sure, we dusted off some things, did a little straightening up in case we have company. Just don't look up under the rug. Don't open the dishwasher. Certainly, don't open the closet. Our truth might come out. MESS. My Embarrassing Shameful Situation.*

5. **Lastly, you're fighting an uphill battle because of the people you keep in your space.** *If you have a house full of small kids, it's highly unlikely that your house will ever be spotless. Think about that same concept when it comes to your life. If you keep people around you that are like children mentally, spiritually, financially and emotionally, you'll never have a clean environment. Why? Children walk in entitlement – they often think that you, along with the rest of the world, owes them something. They're always getting dirty. Always fighting. Competing for attention. Constantly bored or dissatisfied. Ungrateful and unappreciative. Take a moment and think of the people that you allow to live in your space. Are they really entitled, spoiled, contrary, unhappy, disruptive, mean kids masquerading as adult friends? If so, you may have just discovered the reason for some of your mess.*

Now, here's the beauty of how God turns MESS into Miracles. I like to refer to it as a plot twist! In Mark 8:22-26, there's a story about a blind man that is brought to Jesus so that his sight was restored. This man was in a mess! I begin to understand that Jesus was giving us a strategy for turning things around. I'm going to share this with you.

1. **He gets us away from the familiar.** *The first thing that Jesus does is get the blind man by the hand and lead him out of town. What am I saying? When God gets ready to turn things all the way around, He has to ISOLATE us. Why? You can't HEAL in the same place you got SICK.*

2. **He watches how we handle opposition.** *The next thing Jesus does is spit in this man's eyes. Can you imagine that? Spit. Something that's seen in some cultures as one of the most derogatory things that you can do to another human being. Here's the amazing thing. Then blind man doesn't start fighting, cursing or abandoning his chance at healing because he realized something. Sometimes the opportunity is in the opposition! The very thing that came to steal our happiness, strength, sanity and integrity is that thing that God has assigned to release our prosperity, power, peace and position.*

3. **He wants to know if we can finally be honest.** *After spitting in his eyes, Jesus asks the blind man about his vision. The man replies that even though he can see, the people look like trees walking around. What's the significance here? In John 8:32, the bible says that when you know the truth, that truth will set you free. I've discovered that before the truth can set you free, you need to recognize which lies are holding you hostage. Can you stand to tell the truth about how you really feel about your coworker, your pastor, your mother, your siblings, even your children? Sometimes we stay in our mess because we won't tell the truth about what we SEE. We see the lies, the hurt, and the façade but we choose to ignore it. I have a saying: God can't HEAL what you won't REVEAL.*

4. **He needs us to look UP.** *Jesus once again puts his hands on the blind man's eyes but then asks him to look up. The bible says, "and when he was restored, he saw every man clearly." Sometimes, the reason we're not able to see our miracles manifested is because we're looking too*

LOW. We must learn to take the high road. Every response doesn't require our reaction. I have another saying (I'm full of them) that says, "It's not that I can't CLAP BACK, it's just that I'm using my HANDS to BUILD." If you want to see God TURN your situation all the way around, stop looking at the people around you, stop trying to see through the spit that life has thrown in your face. Look unto Jesus, the author & finisher of your faith.

5. **He expects us to move forward.** *The very last thing that Jesus does is to send the formerly blind man to his OWN house and warns him to not only go back into town, but not to even tell anyone in the town what happened. What am I saying? Sometimes the reason God's "turning" can't manifest in our lives is because we keep going back into what He pulled us out of. You can't move forward looking back. Not only are we going back to the wrong people and situations, we keep telling the wrong people about what God is doing in our lives. The joy killers. The pessimists. The narcissists. The haters. The nay-sayers. People that will only bring us back to a state of blindness and right back into MESS. I have a saying (of course I do) that my PAST has PASSED. Let go and grow.*

Now, as I look at where I am now - a beautiful marriage, grown, stable children, the house, cars and career that I dreamed of – I clearly see that God miraculously turned **My E**mbarrassing **S**hameful **S**ituation into **My E**xtraordinary **S**uccess **S**tory. Yes, I'm still a MESS. But God turned it all the way around for my good.

Elisa a writer in the truest sense of the word - she loves words. She's married to Keith and has three children: Latrell, Lex, and Mychal. She is known as Elisa LaShell: The Empowerment Specialist® and uses her creative, expressive gifts to impact both locally and abroad. She loves to travel, learn, share, challenge and inspire. Elisa believes you should never stop trying, never stop loving, and never stop learning.

Study to Show Thyself

CORETTA E. PITTERS

I've always understood "Study to show yourself approved unto God," in 2 Timothy 2:15 (KJV), as it relates to the remainder of the verse, "a worker who does not need to be ashamed, rightly dividing the word of truth." And that's to commit oneself to the study and discernment of God's Word through reading, meditation and prayer, which I assume is most believers' understanding of this passage. However, an encounter with God in summer 2016 revealed a greater discernment of what it means to "Study to show yourself."

After more than a year of trying to decide and discern the area in which I should focus while earning a doctoral degree in nursing, I promised God on the morning of July 15, 2016, that if He provided the way, I would attend seminary. I didn't understand the reason for feeling the I had for weeks leading up to that moment, except that it felt the same as the intense spiritual "tugging" I felt before ultimately answering God's call on my life as a minister in October 2013.

I had planned to set aside some time for meditation and relaxation while attending my sorority's conference, but by then the "tugging" was so strong that I resolved to not run as I had so many years prior to 2013, but rather to immediately surrender to what God obviously was doing and seek His presence. I isolated myself in my hotel room, away from the fellowship and festivities of more than 20,000 of my sorority sisters who were gathered in

Atlanta, GA for our 2016 Boule, and committed to a time of prayer and communion with God, to seek His face AND to hear from Him.

I didn't really know what to ask God or what to pray for. I didn't understand the unreadiness I was feeling, so how could I know what to pray. As a nurse practitioner I was earning a very good salary, and even though I was a divorced single parent at the time, God had allowed provisions for all mine and my two daughters' material needs, and much of the things we desired as well. I was healthy and had no petitions for healing at the time either. And though I didn't know what to pray for, I knew I needed to pray! I did: *"Lord I don't understand what this is, or why I'm feeling this way, or even how to explain what it is I'm feeling."* And, not knowing what to pray, that was my prayer.

After remaining on my knees for some time (how long I don't remember), I said "Amen." I returned to my bed and began reading, *Stories from Inner Space: Confessions of a Preacher Woman and Other Tales,* by Rev. Dr. Claudette Anderson. I had purchased the book earlier in the week, after hearing her powerful sermon at our conference's ecumenical worship service. I had barely made it pass the introductory chapter, when my tears began to flow, honestly more like pour (and crying is something I just don't do much).

The tears poured not because of what I read inside her book, but of what was inside of me, and about to come out. I whispered to the Lord, *"If You provide the way Lord, I'll go to seminary."* In that moment I didn't think of how I would afford it, what sacrifices I would have to make, or what my family and friends would think, not even my daughters, the true "loves of my life."

It scared me, because I had no desire to go to seminary, I had plans to get my doctoral degree in nursing! And, to this day, of which I am currently a second-year Master of Divinity student at the Interdenominational Theological Center (ITC) seminary, I still don't know where those words came from! Surely the Holy Spirit made intercessions for me "with groanings which cannot be uttered...," when I knew not what to pray.

For, though I did not consciously desire to attend seminary, I did desire to please the Lord, and I've learned that if you truly "delight yourself in the Lord, he will give you the desires of your heart," even when you don't know what those desires are.

So, if I didn't desire to attend seminary, then why am I? It would sound good to say to become well-versed and studious in the Word of the Lord, but since it was God not I who called me as a minister, I have resolved in my spirit that if He called me to preach His Word, He has already gifted me with it, I just have to "stir it up." And, if you're thinking as some that it is to some achieve some church or pulpit status, or ordination requirement? It is not!

I have no desire, vision or plan to be a pastor or anything of the such! No Ma'am! No Sir! I study at the Interdenominational Theological Center simply, unadulterated, and completely because this is where God has led me! No, ecclesiastical standing nor the respect or reputation associated with it could motivate me, at this stage of my life, having experienced hardship as well as material and social prosperity, to work half the day as a nurse practitioner and drive roundtrip nearly 400 miles every week to class in Atlanta as I do! But a yearning to please God can and does motivate me.

It's difficult for many to receive that…but one day, I don't remember exactly which one (I didn't write it down, but it's marked on my heart), I realized that everything that I am, everything that I have, and everything I am to be is for the glory of God! I was created by Him, in Him and for Him! I'd fooled around too long, I'd been too relaxed, nonchalant about the things of God concerning my life, and yes, I'd taken His grace and mercy that had covered and protected my life for granted! But thanks be to God, I stopped running from His calling on my life and started running to it! I've sinned and fallen short of His glory too many times to count, yet in my weakness, and seemingly in my most vulnerable times, He has been faithful to uphold me with His hand and has ordered my steps as He did on July 15, 2018.

I had never heard or seen the Rev. Jorethea McCall Capers, who happen to sit next to me in the only empty seat at the table, and one of the few empty seats among the 10,000 in the room at our sorority's Dinner Gala, the very same evening of which I had promised God I'd go to seminary. This obvious vessel of the Lord and a powerful instrument of the Holy Spirit, who mysteriously demonstrated a discerning spirit about me and our conversation as if we had met before, provided God's clear answer to my prayer (my prayer submitted just that morning, of which I knew not what to pray, which could not be uttered...) and helped reveal the next step in God's plan for my life, that of attending seminary rather than pursuing a doctoral degree in nursing. It was not strange that she introduced herself as a retired United Methodist pastor, but it was quite peculiar that she saw fit to mention without any prompting that she attended seminary at ITC, except that it was said for the purpose of my hearing.

I left the after-dinner festivities early and eagerly returned to my hotel room to take a look at ITC and was simply amazed by how compatible this school was to my current life, yet I was even more amazed at how promptly God had answered my prayer, and the tears began to pour again. Within three weeks of this encounter, I was admitted to ITC and began my journey as a seminarian the following Spring 2017 term, but this particular journey to "study to show yourself," for me began when I wholly, unashamedly surrendered to God on the morning of July 15, 2016.

For to study to show yourself approved unto God I've come to understand is being diligent to surrender yourself, your life and yes your heart's desires to be used by God, as a worker "rightly dividing the Word of truth," as demonstrated not only by your knowledge of scripture, but by your walk with Christ. To "study to show yourself," is saying "YES LORD I WILL...," without asking "why, how long or how much," it will take.

However, I've also learned that when you REALLY surrender to God, He'll reveal the answers to all those questions, in His timing. Since beginning seminary, not only have I not been burdened by any school-related debt, but I've been blessed with a higher salaried job and an employer who is sympathetic and accommodating to the demands and challenges of seminary. Every door that has been opened, every financial reward that I've been blessed with (including three thus far), every unexpected check (like the one from the IRS in my mail box last week), every class scheduling resolution, the provisions for my child's care in my absence, and the ability to do exceedingly and abundantly well in all of my courses, including those that have been extremely challenging and those I have absolutely no interest in (smile)... EVERY step has been ordered and directed by the hand of God! You see, when you're diligent to present yourself approved unto God, sometimes He'll do the "studying" for you (*Hallelujah!*).

Minister Coretta Pitters is the proud mother of two beautiful, brilliant daughters, Amari and Taylor. She shares her God-given gifts as Nurse Practitioner, youth mentor advocate, community volunteer, as well as dance and prison ministry. Coretta is a member of Alpha Kappa Alpha Sorority Inc. and a current Master of Divinity student at the Interdenominational Theological Center in Atlanta. Everything is ministry to Coretta but her contentment and greater impact are with youth and young adults, a calling God has confirmed and one she has answered. She strives to walk in His will and purpose for her life by reflecting back the matchless Glory of God at her church home Reaching the Remnant Ministries, and every traditional and non-conventional ministry setting to which God calls her.

I Don't Look Like What I Went Through

Victory Lowe

It was June 7, 2016, when I went to Family Practices doctor's office on the Maxwell Air Force Base in Montgomery, Alabama, for lab work. On June 14th, I was informed of my results, and it was not good news at all. My liver enzyme levels were high. I had an ultrasound so that my physicians could provide a sound diagnosis. That test indicated I had diffuse infiltrates of the liver. From there, I was immediately referred to the Jackson Imaging Center to have a magnetic resonance imaging (MRI) conducted to determine the extent of damage to my liver . . .

Just a couple days later a sweet physician's assistant, Candace, telephoned and requested me to report to Family Practices for my MRI results. For some reason, I felt in my spirit the results were not good. That feeling was right. I was told that the MRI revealed numerous large lesions throughout the liver that was compatible with metastatic disease: cancer. Things seemed to move so quickly from that point forward.

On June 27th, I had an appointment with Dr. Strickland to have a biopsy. The biopsy indicated I had breast cancer. This horrific news took me to a very deep, dark place. I really didn't know what to do, so I called on Jesus to heal me. In Isaiah 53:5, His word says, *"But He was wounded for our transgressions, He was bruised for our iniquities; the chastisement for our peace was upon Him, and by His stripes we are healed."*(NIV)

Subsequently, Candace referred me to Dr. John Reardon and scheduled an appointment for me to see him on July 7th at the Montgomery Cancer

Center. Things moved very quickly again. The very next day, Dr. Reardon conducted a positron emission tomography (PET) scan. On July 9th, my husband Bobby and I went to get the PET scan results. My pastor, Dr. Wendy Coleman, and best friend, Laine Petters, also came to give their moral and spiritual support.

The PET scan revealed I had stage 4 metastatic breast cancer (MBC), meaning the breast cancer had metastasized (spread) to the liver, spine, pelvis bone, and lymph nodes – practically all over my body. In fact, I had so many tumors that they could not even get an exact marker reading. However, when they finally got a marker reading, it was 18,000 plus!

Dr. Reardon recommended that I immediately start chemo treatments. My first treatment was on July 13th, and Bobby was right there beside me. I was a little afraid, but I prayed. The Lord told me, *"For God did not give us a spirit of fear, but of power, and of love and of a sound mind"* (2 Timothy 1:7 NIV). After the first three months of chemo treatments, the cancer was gone from all areas in my body, except in the bones, and I give God all the praise and glory. *Hallelujah*!

My hallelujah is genuine because when I tell my testimony, some people can't believe it. During the weeks of treatment, many said, "You don't look like someone going through chemo." I said it was only by God's grace and mercy because I have been on several types of chemo. For instance, on May 4, 2018, I started a new chemo called Ixempra. The first dose was too strong. It depleted my blood, platelets, and calcium. I was in the hospital for six days, and I can say now I didn't know if I would make it out because the medicine made me so sick. But I haven't been "sick" – from the cancer - since I was diagnosed.

Are you ready to shout? As of September 28, 2018, my tumor markers are 424.4, and I give all the praise and glory to God! I almost died, but God said, *"Not so!"* Prophetess VaNessa Sykes, my niece and a pastor, said she was driving home on this specific day when the Lord told her to call her mother, Betty Sykes, who is also my sister, to pray away the death angels. They prayed steadfastly until they got a release. At that time, I was rejuvenated by God's grace and mercy and the prayers of the righteous ones. In James 5:16, "*The effectual fervent prayers of the righteous avail much*" (NIV). I'm a living witness to that truth.

God told me I have purposes to fulfill: one is to worship Him and serve His people; the other one is to tell my testimony of how He healed me. His purpose for healing me was not for me to go back in the world: He healed me to set me apart. I am His chosen vessel for Him to live through and to use.

Evidently, when the devil can't get you in one area of the body, he will attack another area. What the devil doesn't know is that I am covered by the blood of Jesus! As the tumor markers continue to decrease, and I have had radiation on my brain twice because there were two spots found there. The first radiation treatment was on April 6, 2018, which eliminated the spot. The second radiation treatment was on September 27, 2018. I believe it will also work in my favor!

On January 18, 2019, I had a scan and got my results on January 25th. The results were super great! My tumor markers were so low that chemo was stopped. However, if any chance my tumor markers go back up for two consecutive months, Dr, Reardon stated that he would restart chemo. But I decree in the name of Jesus that they will not go back up. Hallelujah!

I refused to let a cancer diagnosis stop me from doing the things I wanted to do with my family. That positive outlook – along with faith & prayer – plays a major part in fighting and winning this battle. I thank God for the people who walk with me on this journey: my husband, Dr. Bobby Lowe; sons, Derrick & Tyler; my pastor; mother-in-law, Lizzie Lowe; friends, Laine Pitters & Georgia Kuffman; sisters, Betty Bridges, Linda Jackson, & Martha Pennington; niece, VaNessa Young; brother, Johnny Orr; and sister-in-law, Sarah Orr.

*I also thank God for His healing power. I have faith, and I am expecting complete healing because that's what His word says in Jeremiah 30:17, "**For I will restore health to you and heal you of your wounds**"(NIV). I thank*

You, Lord, that I have overcome sickness and disease by the blood of the Lamb and the word of my testimony. To God be the glory!

Victory was born to Jimmy Pittin & Viola Carvin in Humboldt, TN, grew up in Vernon, Alabama, graduated from Vernon Lamar HS. She earned her Assoc. Degree in Business Admin. from Troy Univ. Victory is an Ordained Deacon and faithful member at Reaching the Remnant Ministries. She's been married to her soulmate and best friend, Bobby, 37 years. They have two sons, Derrick and Tyler, and one amazing grandson, Dallas. Victory is a retiree of banking for 28 years.

Her motto is "I can do all things through Christ who strengthens me."

He Did It Before, He'll Do It Again

BETTY BRIDGES

Jeremiah 29:11
*For I know the thoughts that I think toward you, saith Jehovah, thoughts
of peace, and not of evil, to give you hope in your latter end.* (NIV)

Proverbs 19:21
*Many are the plans in the mind of a man, but it is the
purpose of the LORD that will stand.* (NIV)

A basic need of every human being is to love and be loved. It is my sincere
expectation that this article will help single young ladies who desire to be
married not to make choices that will delay God's plans for their lives and
that it will give hope for the more mature single ladies. In a small town
in Alabama in 1956 at the age of 10, a handsome, tall, lanky young boy
(Jerry) caught my attention and ignited a "puppy love" fire in my heart.
Little did I know that the fire would never be completely extinguished,
but due to life's choices, for a season would be *"banked"* (*the process of
restricting the flow of air to a fire by piling ashes around or over embers so
that they can be easily revived at a later time*). As I grew older, my feelings
for Jerry grew as well.

Two years later three life changing events occurred: (1) I accepted Jesus
Christ as my Lord and Savior. (2) Puppy love for Jerry began transitioning
into a more mature love that I knew even at that young age was real. (3) I
was entering junior high school. At this time my mother issued an edict,
"don't let any boy touch you so that you can graduate from high school."

An edict without an explanation, grace and trust is destined to bring about heartache and failure. The edict was enforced by not allowing me the freedom to date. The irony is that as far back as I can remember, my mother had told me that Jerry and I were going to be married. Although I was not allowed to spend any time with him, I never discounted my mother's "prophecy" because of how I felt for him.

The shift: What happened next altered both my and Jerry's lives for the next one-half century. Throughout history, failure to communicate and/or poor communication has led to heartache, discouragement and even war and death. I assumed I was Jerry's "special" girlfriend and that we were destined for marriage. He assumed he was not "suitable" for me in the eyes of my parents and pursued other relationships. When I became aware of some of the choices he'd made and the consequences, it was as if a huge dagger had been plunged into my heart. The pain I felt was indescribable. In an attempt to ease my pain, my mother said that Jerry did not deserve me.

What now? The young man who I began loving as a very young girl was no longer a marriage prospect, untouched physically by a man yet with no knowledge of how to discern the motives of young men. Is it now okay to be "touched"? Rebounding from a lost love and wanting to feel wanted and loved after the "loss" of the young man that I really loved and wanted, I made a choice that had disastrous consequences, compounded by marrying and moving to Ohio.

Part of my daily prayer was, *"Lord before I come home to be with you, I would like to experience the love of a man that loves you with all of his heart."* Yearly I returned to my small hometown in Alabama and for the first 22 years, Jerry and I communicated briefly just to say hello and wish each other well. We respected each other's marital status and the call on his life in ministry, but there was no denying that we still loved each other.

After 30 years of not seeing or talking to each other, in November 2017, I was informed that Jerry was now a widower. I had been a widow for 13 years. I vacillated between sympathy for him while wondering if our relationship could be rekindled after 60 years. After conferring with my pastor, I called him. As soon as I heard his voice, I knew I still loved him, yet I was unable to discern what he was feeling. Because of that, I was very vague about when I would be in Alabama again.

The Revival: At his request, I attended a ministry celebration in his honor. When I laid eyes on him for the first time after 30 years, it was as though God took a special key, went into a secret chamber of my heart and released a flow of love for Jerry with an intensity like none I have ever experienced.

At Last: On April 6, 2018 at 12 noon in Gatlinburg, TN at age 72, a man I had loved most of my life who I know was appointed, anointed and chosen by God to love me as I had never been loved before, became my husband. Daily we are in awe of what God is doing in and through us and we know that our marriage is not **about** us, but it **is** for our good but more importantly, God's glory in kingdom building. We are both happier than we have ever been and are enjoying latter days' blessings in accordance with **Job 8:7** and **Song of Solomon** is one of our favorite books of the bible (if you catch my drift).

Ladies, (young, mature, saved and unsaved) God has a plan for your lives and it is the very best. Position yourselves to receive it. You see, although there might be many people suitable to be one's spouse, only the one chosen by God will be the BEST!! He brought us together 62 years ago and He brought us back together 62 years later.

Betty is the proud mother of 3, grandmother of 6 and great grandmother of 1, all of whom make her life rich. Her marriage blessed her with 3 bonus sons and 4 bonus grandchildren who have enriched her life even more. She is also an ordained elder and graduate of Ashland Theological Seminary. At 72, after being widowed for 13 years, this newlywed reunited with her sweetheart. She & Pastor Jerry Bridges  *were joined in holy matrimony on April 6, 2018. Betty is currently being used by God to teach and equip women to utilize their God-given gifts and talents.*

A Blessed Life: The Gift of Spreading the Gospel Through Music

ANGIER STEWART JOHNSON

Mic Check! Testing 1, 2, 3 is the standard on air check for on-air broadcasters. This life has been just that, a test preparing me for and where I am today: abundantly Blessed! Who would have thought my hair-brained idea for reading public service announcements as a resume builder, would result to a job offer at a low-powered AM signal and, 29-years later, would further advance to affording me a radio presence on not one, but two FM signals in the Montgomery market. Nobody but God!

Mic Check! Testing 1, 2, 3! Early years of radio were not glamorous by any stretch of the imagination. There I was, weighing a buck and change, getting up on Saturday mornings to sign-on at 5:00 am in a creepy building sitting in the middle of a field in Wetumpka, going to get my radio game on. It was 1989 and I was a newlywed. My hubby had NO interest in the cracking that exude from the radio, regardless of if it was his wife or someone else's. He just had no interest. I looked for him to be my cheerleader and say, "Good Job!" That was my interest all by myself, so I had to find encouragement and the "Atta Boys," on my own ultimately encouraging myself. The years progressed and from there, we add a cow field to our resume. I did not stutter, and you read correctly, "cow field," is exactly what I said!

My first FM radio gig was WSFU in Union Springs, Alabama. The signal was bananas and you couldn't tell us nothing! I worked the AM station on Saturday mornings and my new FM in Union Springs on Sundays. I was voice-tracking back in the day before voice-tracking became a trend. I would make my trek to the station in Union Springs and would record a week's worth of shows to cassette. The tapes were played the entire week, and no one knew that I wasn't present in a studio where the transmitter sat smack in the middle of the field. Hilarious! We kept the music current and the praise fresh and the listeners loved this new sound and the new female air talent. "Humble beginnings" is an understatement, wouldn't you say?

Mick Check! Testing 1, 2,3! Blest the Lord! Oh, My Soul! WVAS-FM 90.7 The Voice of Alabama State University! The station positioned on the beautiful campus of ASU was 80,000 watts of power, covering 27 Alabama counties. I had died and landed in Heaven but was literally too crazy to see what a "blessing" God had entrusted to me. There was no gospel programming in the dawn and the management initially told me, there was no funds to offer me a contract. The station was running a pre-recorded program. The music shelves were empty. There was no music.

I took my little hard-earned tokens and purchased music to play on the air, to the strong opposition of the Mister. He definitely had reason to oppose! We were a young married couple with a young baby, struggling to make ends meet. My charitable deed to radio was literally food being taken out of our mouths. Lol! I often found so much inspiration from the gospel music, so I wanted to share that same feeling with my listeners. One Sunday, shortly after I had gone on the air, Mel Marshall, one of the popular on-air personalities, called me and said that he was listening. He complimented me on my selection of music and stated that he was really touched. He said it seemed from listening that each music track played that morning had a message in the song. From that conversation, he gave me my radio handle, "The Gospel Messenger."

Many Sundays, I felt no one was listening and I wanted to throw in the towel. It was my dear Mother's counsel who cautioned me not to grow "weary in well doing." I can remember her telling me how I would never imagine the lives I was touching via the airwaves on Sundays. Right Ma! *Ain't no phone ringing. I'm sitting here playing music for no one but me.* I thought to myself, *was she really my Mom, or Job's wife because she was talking foolish*! Well, to my amazement, she must have been on to something. I couldn't keep up with the volume of calls, we begin to receive on Sundays. I begin to go to the grocery store and as I wrote a check for my grocery order, the cashier would recognize my name and say, "I listen to you on Sundays on WVAS! I love your variety of music! It really gets me ready for church!" I would turn around to see if she was talking about someone else. Certainly, she's not talking about me.

I was honored but more so humbled! There were other options for gospel radio, and she thought enough to listen to me? Wow! That's not all! The calls and letters and requests begin to pour in. Inmates from both the male and female penal facilities, making requests and looking to hear their names on Sundays. Some would even have the wardens and correctional officers to call me with their list of favorites and shout-outs.

Of the many accounts, I think the one with the guy who would be my first caller every Sunday. How about we just call him Ricky, ok? I would sign-on at 6:00 am and it never failed that before I could close my microphone with my morning's opening, the telephone is ringing, and it was Ricky. Lord knows, most mornings I would be in a rushed frenzy trying to make it to the station on time. Sometimes, it would become frustrating because I would just be starting my air shift and attempting to organize music, run the broadcast board and answer the telephone and there was Ricky up for a lengthy conversation.

In spite of any frustration, I wasn't rude to him and always made time to just listen. He was super intelligent, but I would often wonder why he was up so early in the morning. Several years passed and it seemed he fell off the face of the earth. Mind you, we had never met, as with many of my listeners, if they walked up to me, I wouldn't know them. Yet, you really feel like they are extended family and that's exactly how they feel about you too. You hear all about what's going on with their families and begin to know them too by name. You literally hear it all!

One day I was at my fulltime job, which was on the campus in another department and I received a call transferred from the radio station to my office. The voice sound familiar but I didn't know who it was. What do you know? It was Ricky, calling to thank me. I asked for what? He gave me his powerful testimony of how he had been delivered from personal issues.

He went on to explain to me when I received those early morning calls (the first one each Sunday). I couldn't remember but he told me that each Sunday he would request the exact same song. He said that I had no idea how the music and my taking time to talk with him served as a source of inspiration to him. He shared that he had gone to seek help and was clean and had totally turned his life around. Mic Check! Test 1, 2, 3! Glory!!! What A Testimony!

Through my gospel music ministry, I have been blessed. I often hear what a blessing I am on Sundays. Oh no, I am truly the beneficiary of the abundance of blessings that God has showered upon me. In the early years, my commitment was unwavering in my assignment as the gospel personality on WVAS-FM. There were many, many Sundays that I was at the station with my boys in tow. I would bring church clothes, blankets, the cereal and the milk. I would get the boys dressed in between songs and then I would get prepared and off to the house of prayer we would go. Talkin' about multi-tasking. A Mama does what she has to do! Nonetheless, we got it done!

Mic Check! Testing 1,2,3! There has been so much that has transpired over the years…. Marriage, motherhood, divorce, the loss of my Dad and illness. I guess I should preface my next thought by saying this. It is easier to preach ten sermons than it is to live one. For over two decades now, I have been known as the "Gospel Messenger," hosting Sunday Morning Gospel for WVAS-FM 90.7 which reaches thousands of gospel enthusiasts weekly. My main mission in my radio career has been to uplift, encourage, and inspire my listening audience by offering insight to the Gospel also known as "The Good News." Yet, the news that I got late May of 2005, left me in a position to where I immediately had to practice what I preached.

One Thursday afternoon, after a routine mammogram, I was summoned to return to the Montgomery Breast Center to hear, "You have breast cancer." Accompanied by my mother, I was stunned to hear the news. I stared straight ahead and felt totally lifeless. I was thinking, "This is a bad dream, a nightmare, and I just need to wake up." A recent divorcee, my mind fell to my two young sons. I thought, "They need me!"

That became the "it" factor. I prayed for God to spare my life, to allow me to see them complete school and become men. I asked Him if he would be so kind to allow me to see future generations….. some grands and great-grands, if He pleased. My boys gave me the will to survive, to live, to fight and to beat the monster that had invaded my body. With a doctor and nurse standing by, holding a Kleenex for me, I asked, "What's next?"

Because I knew time was of the essence, within an hour, I had chosen an oncologist and a surgeon and immediately started putting my treatment plan into action that same afternoon. The next few days: Pre-op Friday, I spoke at my sister-in-law's funeral Saturday (who by the way had died from complications of breast cancer). While comforting my sons, I returned home from her funeral to tell them their Mom had cancer too! I worked my air shift that Sunday morning at the radio station and the next day had surgery, followed by 42 radiation treatments over the next several months.

For six years, I took daily doses of the drug Tamoxifen, a protocol for blocking breast cancer but it could cause uterine cancer. Since our focus is on blessings, Praise God, I made it through the hot flashes and night sweats brought on by this drug – lol! Thank God the Tamoxifen followed by the drug Aromasin are in my rear-view mirror. Aromosin was not quite as dangerous. I lived with the ongoing joint pain for a few years but survived it too.

In all honesty, back then, I couldn't have done what I'm doing today. I wanted nothing to do with the pink ribbons or anything associated with Cancer and its research. To me, becoming involved was a reminder of something I wanted to forget happened. I quickly realized, I was so wrong and asked God for forgiveness. I know that it was God that quickened my spirit and reminded me that it was "He" that had spared me: not so much for me, but so that I could be a blessing to someone else through my testimony of his unyielding mercy.

My role as a messenger doesn't just come upon me during October (Breast Cancer Awareness Month), but at every opportunity, with audiences large or small, I share my personal experience and message of hope to inspire others. I mean after all of my years of being the Gospel Messenger, beating breast cancer shed new light to the familiar scripture in Revelations, "We are overcome by the blood of the lamb and the words of our testimony! Hmm . . . Cancer, the test!! Angier, the testimony!!

Mic Check! Testing 1,2,3! One of my favorite quotes is by Regina Britt. It simply says, "Life isn't tied with a bow, but it's still a gift!" I'm so grateful for the gift of life. My perspective on life has changed in so many ways. Things that use to weigh heavily in importance has lessened in value, such as birthdays, gifts, material things and the like. When I open my eyes and see that God has "gifted" me with a new day, that truly feels like Christmas and my birthday.

An extension of that blessing is when I have my annual mammogram and the report is clear, this girl is truly on top of the world. To say that God is good and I am blessed is an understatement. Today I burst with pride over two little people who refer to me as their MiMi! Let me tell you, I thought motherhood was good but being a grandparent is like life, the best thing going! That is strong indicator that God honored and answered my prayers and as the "Messenger," my message is stronger as I strive for excellence in Christ. As I end this writing that briefly documents my journey of being the Gospel Messenger, I am humbled by the fact that I would never be the woman I am today without He who gave me purpose and for those who came on this journey with me.

Angier Johnson is a veteran radio announcer in the Montgomery area. She can be heard on the airwaves of WVAS-FM 90.7, hosting Sunday Morning Gospel from 6-11 am. Additionally, join her daily as "AJ in the Midday" with the Gospel Café, 10 am until 2 pm on PRAISE 96.5 FM.

God Still Has the Final Word

LaToya Williams Bell

As we go through life, we make our own plans for the things we envision for our present and our future. We plan to live carefree lives that will go on with no problems or trials. I, too, had these plans and dreams of carefree living and just like everyone else, God had the final say on what would really take place in my life.

Life has a funny way of making Proverbs 16:1 a resounding truth- *"We can make our own plans, but the Lord gives the right answer." —NLT.* These are what I like to call "but God" moments. Inevitably, we all experience "but God" moments when we have reached the end of our ropes, when the enemy has made his plan and when giving up seems to be the best option. Recently, I experienced a "but God" moment that gave me a miraculous testimony and the confidence to say, "God *STILL* has the final word."

"It's that time again," I thought to myself as I began to check my breasts for lumps just as I had been taught to do each month. Hoping and expecting I would not find anything, I was alarmed when I saw an unusual secretion. Immediately, I called my doctor for an appointment. As I sat in my doctor's office, listening for my name to be called, what had to be several million thoughts swarmed my mind. "We don't have a history of breast cancer." "But I didn't feel any lumps." "Oh, God, did I miss a lump?" "I'm too young to die."

Thirty years old and thinking about my own funeral was beginning to stress me out. When I heard the nurse call my name, I began to take deep

52

breaths. As I undressed, I could feel the pitter patter of my heart grow into deafening thuds. I leaned back as instructed and the exam by my doctor began. What I heard next was so unexpected; those loud thuds became a vacuum of silence. "I'm sending you to get an MRI, I think you have a tumor on your brain," my doctor said. So matter-of-fact, so cold were her words that I did not feel anything a numbness and a vastness that parallels sensory deprivation came over me.

Where was God? Had I not been faithful enough? Had I not been good enough? Had I not repented for my sins with sincerity? I knew I heard from God frequently, but where was he now? With tears hotly streaming down my face, I tried to focus on the words coming out of the scheduling nurse's mouth. I struggled to take the MRI appointment card she handed me.

I walked out of that office with my head hung in shame. Shame that radiated from a place of fear. The devil was wreaking havoc on my soul with the mental warfare. There I was, a "First Lady", a "preacher's kid", a "minister" in my own right allowing the enemy to defeat me. Never once did I think about the God I served. Never once did I think of Proverbs 16. Fortunately, God does not stop what He does because we forget who He is. God *STILL* has the final word.

Days have passed now, as I roamed around in a zombie-like state, asking for prayer, utterly defeated. I climbed onto the MRI table and prayed. Silent weeps escaped my closed eyelids and gently parted lips. The nurses checked on me and I insisted I was fine; but truthfully, I had given up. I had forgotten the words taught to me, "You can give out, but don't you give up!" As the MRI continued, the contrast from the IV made me so nauseated they could barely finish the test. Nevertheless, I finished the test and went home to wallow some more. The phone rung three days later, "We have your results, can you please come in?"

This doctor's visit was different that the last. I did not feel anxious or any emotion for that matter. I walked back to my doctor's office and she had a puzzled look on her face. I hung my head expecting the worse. "There was nothing there," she said. "I don't understand. Your blood levels and the secretion were all the indications of a tumor on your Pituitary gland. There should be something here!" Just like that, I had my "but God" moment. "Did you think I would fail you?" "Did you think I'd remove my hand from the vessel I created?" "Did you think I was done with what I created you for?"

"Did you think I wouldn't have the FINAL WORD?" "I am God." "I am the doctor who never lost a patient." "I Am that I Am." "I will never leave you, nor forsake you." For every negative thought I had and discouraging word I heard in that same doctor's office, God canceled them all. He reminded me that no matter what, He *STILL* has the FINAL WORD!

LaToya is a servant leader who provides her clients with zealous advocacy and compassionate service. She is an Assistant Public Defender in the Houston Judicial Circuit Public Defender's Office in Warner Robins, Georgia. She is also an adjunct professor at Central Georgia Technical College. She is the wife of Overseer Eric Bell and bonus mom of three: Breanna, Tamarius and Zackary. She enjoys cooking, baking, crafting and decorating.

P-U-S-H

STEPHANIE LEWIS-PROVITT

In 1988, I gave my life to Christ and thought all my problems would go away. However, it was the total opposite. I was in a relationship and my engagement however, ended abruptly. It seemed like everyone started getting married all around me as I was just coming out of a relationship. I was happy for my friends however, I said, *"Lord what about me?"* God knows the end from the beginning, and he knew that I wasn't ready for marriage at that time. I thought that I was, I knew how to cook, iron, sew, etc. However, there's much more to being a wife.

I shared how I felt with a sister in the Lord and her advice was, "Stephanie, guys chase a girl until the girl catches him. In other words, he's going to come looking for you because God word is true that says, *Whosoever findeth a wife findeth a good thing and receiveth favor of the Lord* (Proverbs 18:22 NIV)." God's word is so true, I began to seek after God with my whole heart and everything that was within me. I joined the praise team, began ministering at the prisons, and became active in the single's ministry. God had to work some things out of me to prepare me to be a wife. When I stop searching, he found me.

I was at a singles conference in the early part of 1991 and met a young man named Samuel Ellis Provitt. I didn't think that he was interested in me, so I tried to introduce him to other ladies in the church. We became friends and he wasn't interested in anybody but me. So, one day he asked me out on a date.

I knew that I wasn't interested in him, so I didn't dress to part. I didn't fix my hair in any special way and I had holes in my jeans. And yet, he still was interested in little ole me. He still pursued me and told me that God said that I was going to be his wife. He asked me to marry him. I told him no. I told him that God didn't tell me that!

I kept serving and running after God with everything in me. Finally, he asked me again. I told him that I had to pray about it. Proverbs 3:6 say *in all your ways acknowledge Him, and He shall direct your paths (NKJV)*. Once I acknowledged God about it, he put a yes in my spirit and I told Samuel yes, I will marry you. God will give you double for your trouble when you wait on him because I got a man after God's own heart and good-looking man too!

After one year in the marriage, my desire was to have a child. That's when the battle started in my mind. The enemy fought me so hard and told me boldly that I wasn't going to have any children and I kind of believed him because I miscarried with my first and third pregnancy. That was one of the few things in life that devastated my hope and destroyed my joy. I knew several of my friends were trying to have children but were unable to even conceive a child.

It was bitterly painful and disappointing, for sure. Carrying a baby in your womb only to discover you will never be able to hold and take care of him or her is another kind of pain and heartache that cuts very deep. It can even cause us to wonder; *Where is God during a miscarriage?* Somehow, I didn't let that stop my belief in what I was believing the Lord for. I know many other couples who have experienced the disappointment of miscarriage, and I've seen some handle it better than others.

I began reading a book titled **Supernatural Childbirth by Jackie Mize**. It encouraged me and built my faith to help me overcome defeat and triumphed in God›s plan for childbirth! Jackie Mize had been told she could never have children. However, by unlocking powerful truths and dynamic faith principles in the Bible, they now have four miracle children! **I was standing on God's word.** What does God say and what does the bible say child birth?

God says we can have children. He said be fruitful and multiply and in Genesis 1: 27-28, the Word declares *"God created man in His own image; in the image of God He created him; male and female He created them. God blessed them and said to them, Be fruitful, multiply, and fill the earth and subdue it; rule over the fish of the sea and the birds of the air and every creature that crawls upon the earth"(NIV.)* I began to understand that God loves me just that much. I realized He has no respect of persons and what he did for Jackie, He would do the same thing for me!

I am proud to now say, "Thank You, Lord, for my three miracle children, Samaria, Caleb and Samequa!" I realized that I had to PUSH: PRAY UNTIL SOMETHING HAPPENED! Sometimes you must get alone and spend that quality time with God. *"And Jacob was left alone; and there wrestled a man with him until the breaking of the day. And when he saw that he prevailed not against him, he touched the hollow of his thigh; and the hollow of Jacob's thigh was out of joint, as he wrestled with him. And he said, Let me go, for the day breaketh. And he said, I will not let thee go, except thou bless me"* (Genesis 32:24-26 NIV).

As you consider my testimony, please don't limit yourself to thinking this is about conceiving, birthing, and raising children. Whatever you are believing the Lord for - a husband, a child, job, house, financial blessing or even just a closer relationship with Him - remember to **PUSH: PRAY UNTIL SOMETHING HAPPENS.**

Stephanie & her husband, Elder Sam Provitt, are the proud parents of three – Samaria, Caleb, Samequa – and recently welcomed their first grandchild, Kai Daniel Larkin. Earning her bachelor's & master's degrees from Alabama State University, she serves as staff associate in the Department of Theatre & Dance there. A faithful, Anointed Woman of God, Stephanie  *is also an ordained elder whose current assignment at Fresh Anointing House of Worship in Montgomery.*

Great is Thy Faithfulness to Me

KEISHA THOMAS

Let us hold fast the profession of our faith without wavering;
*(for **he is faithful** that promised).* Hebrews 10:23 (NIV)

It is of the LORD's mercies that we are not consumed, because
his compassions fail not. They are new every morning:
great is thy faithfulness. Lamentations 3:22-23 (NIV)

My husband and I married in 2002. After a couple years of marriage, we decided to start trying to have a baby. In 2005, I got pregnant but suffered a miscarriage. For many years after this, we were unsuccessful at getting pregnant. We visited doctors and fertility specialists and endured numerous medical tests, procedures, and surgery. However, with each procedure, came disappointment repeatedly.

In 2013, we took a break from the doctors, tests and procedures. To our surprise, September 22nd of that year would prove to be a very special day. A lady who was visiting our church shared her testimony of how God had blessed her with a child when the doctors told her that she could not conceive again. As she was speaking, I identified with what she was saying. I could not help but wonder if I was pregnant (as I was experiencing some unusual things in my body).

After 11 years of marriage and an abundance of effectual, fervent prayers of the righteous, we discovered we were indeed pregnant on the very day we heard the awesome testimony! A few months later, I gave birth to a healthy, joyful baby boy. God had performed a miracle! The doctor even stood in amazement and stated that he did not see how I had gotten pregnant. But God! God did it! As the song goes…*Everything that happened to me that was good, God did it!* God did what doctors could not do, my husband could not do and I could not do. God holds life in His hands!

As I consider this supernatural blessing from God and look at my precious son, I'm often reminded of the Promises of God concerning all the trying moments of life we can face. Will you allow me to share some of them with you? It is my prayer that you, too, will be able to find strength in them.

I. God works in impossible situations. Just know that "It's Possible!" Whatever your "it" is, it is possible! If God wills your "it," it shall be.

James 1:17 *Every good gift and every perfect gift is from above, and cometh down from the Father of lights, with whom is no variableness, neither shadow of turning. (NIV)*

Psalm 127:3 (NLT) *Children are a gift from the LORD; THEY ARE A REWARD FROM HIM.*

Luke 18:27 *And he said, The things which are impossible with men are possible with God. (NIV)*

Luke 1:37 *For with God nothing shall be impossible.* (NKJV)

II. God is not bound by what usually happens. He can stretch the limits and cause supernatural events to occur.

Mark 9:23 *Jesus said unto him, If thou canst believe, all things are possible to him that believeth. (NKJV)*

Jeremiah 32:17 *There is nothing too hard for the Lord. (NIV)*

III. God is reliable. We can trust God to keep His promises.

Ephesians 3:20 (NLT) *Now all glory to God, who is able, through his mighty power at work within us, to accomplish infinitely more than we might ask or think.*

2 Corinthians 1:20 *For all the promises of God in him are yea, and in him Amen, unto the glory of God by us. (NIV)*

Numbers 23:19 *God is not a man, that he should lie; neither the son of man, that he should repent: hath he said, and shall he not do it? or hath he spoken, and shall he not make it good?(NIV)*

IV. God works in perfect His timing. The promise may be "delayed but not denied."

Habakkuk 2:3 *For the vision is yet for an appointed time, but at the end it shall speak, and not lie: though it tarry, wait for it; because it will surely come, it will not tarry. (NIV)*

Isaiah 55:11 *So shall my word be that goeth forth out of my mouth: it shall not return unto me void, but it shall accomplish that which I please, and it shall prosper in the thing whereto I sent it. (NKJV)*

As I conclude our conversation, there's something that I know will bless you as YOU WAIT ON GOD to manifest His fulfilled promises in your life. Let these principles guide you.

1) Rejoice While You Wait. Romans 12:15 *Rejoice with them that do rejoice, and weep with them that weep.* (NIV)

Learn how to rejoice in other's victories. As I waited, I hosted and/or attended several baby showers. I showered others with love and blessings as I waited on my blessing. You reap what you sow. In Luke 1:39-44, Elisabeth rejoiced with Mary who had received word that she would bear a son. Upon hearing the news, Elizabeth's baby leaped in her womb for joy.

2). Work While You Wait. 1 Corinthians 15:58 *Therefore, my beloved brethren, be ye steadfast, unmovable, always abounding in the work of the Lord, forasmuch as ye know that your labor is not in vain in the Lord. (NIV)*

Don't stop doing what God has called you to do while you're waiting. *"Because God has not done this or that for me, I am not going to do this or that for Him."*

Quid pro quo does not apply in the kingdom! We are called to obey God; whether He does what we want Him to do when we want Him to do it or not.

Sometimes God will ask you to do things for the kingdom when the prayers and desires of your heart have not been fulfilled. He wants to know your motives. Will you walk in obedience even though you have not received your blessing and see no visible sign of it in the future? He wants to know if you truly love Him or just what He has to offer. Do you love the blessing more than the Blesser? I experienced a miscarriage in 2005 and was ordained a minister in 2006. God was steadily requiring things of me in ministry and other areas of my life; yet, I still had not received the things I had been praying for. Zacharias, Elisabeth's husband, ministered as priest/servant. He continued to work and pray (Luke 1:8-9). You should not stop what you are doing while you wait. Continue diligently to obey and do what God has called you to do. (NIV)

3). Worship While You Wait. John 4:24 *God is a Spirit: and they that worship him must worship him in spirit and in truth. (NKJV)*

Don't let the delay of blessings hinder your worship or stop your praise. My praise and worship were not hindered by my circumstances; but rather based solely on my love and adoration for God. Remember that God's Faithfulness Does Not Change! What He did for me; He can do for you. Same God! Same Power! Same Faithfulness! *Jesus Christ is the same yesterday and today and forever* (Hebrews 13:8 NKJV).

Keisha D. Thomas wears many hats: wife, mother, daughter, sister, aunt, evangelist, leader, and many more. At an early age, she accepted Jesus Christ as her Lord and Savior. She has a heart to serve the Lord and a will to please Him. She wants her testimony to be like that of Enoch's: that she walks with God and pleases God. Her motto is "Not My Will, but God's Will Be Done."

to be when you need to be there. I have had two occasions (both while travelling for work, ironically) where I encountered a stranger in the midst of a personal crisis—one in the throes of an epileptic attack who passed out in the hallway during a training at a high school; and the other having a legal crisis—a grandmother who was desperately trying to win custody of a grandchild, was denied, and was in the parking lot of the courthouse sprawled out on the hood of her vehicle crying hysterically.

In neither case was I fully aware of the circumstances that led to what I was witnessing. I did the only thing I knew to do: I approached each woman, laid my hand on her, told her that I was a Christian, and asked if I could pray for her. In both instances, each woman said "yes." And relying on what God dropped into my spirit, prayed the most fervent prayer I could muster until the paramedics arrived and moved the epileptic woman onto the stretcher and, respectively, until the distraught grandmother's breathing became calm and steady.

I never learned their names and I don't recall sharing mine. We didn't exchange contact information or agree to "friend" the other on Facebook. I will never know the identity of those women and I will never forget those encounters. Never. I lose nothing by being gracious. I lose nothing by being attentive. I lose nothing by engaging with another person with whom I have no previous affiliation. I lose nothing by showing love to my fellow man. The song goes "The Jesus in me loves the Jesus in you… it's so easy… easy to love." Indeed.

Sometimes someone truly does need a helping hand. This Christmas, my church—Reaching the Remnant Ministries—sponsored women and children at a homeless shelter. In perusing the names to determine the <u>individual</u> for whom I would provide Christmas, I noticed two of the women were in my peer group. Perfect! We're close in age—maybe what I like, they'll like. I also wanted to sponsor <u>one</u> of the children. I noticed there were two 10-year old little girls whose names sounded similar. "They must surely be twins," I thought. But nothing on the provided information gave any indication of siblings or family members. I dedicated myself to shopping for four people. Four strangers in an undesirable situation—two of whom were children—who deserved to have a nice Christmas.

I knew nothing about them but their names, ages, and clothes sizes of the kids. My heart exploded as I bustled around from store to store selecting goodies and needs for these persons. Buying two of everything for the little girls (just in case they were indeed twins) and two of everything for the women (but different colors). I admittedly went overboard; above and beyond what was probably expected. Santa's workshop had nothing on my living room! Clothes and gadgets and trinkets and whatnots everywhere! I remembered my own Christmases as a child about how my mother would wrap our gifts and how excited my sister and I would be to tear off the wrappings and dig in the boxes. It took me two nights to wrap and box, bag and tissue paper every single thing for these four individuals. By the time I was done, I had 4 large industrial-size garbage bags of gifts--one for each person.

I was blessed to be a blessing. "Barak to Barakah", as Pastor Coleman taught in Bible Study. God confirmed for me that what I had done was ordained by him when we delivered the gifts to the shelter: the two little girls were in fact twins; one of the peers that I had chosen happened to be their mother! My God is AWESOME! As I tried to warn her about the sizes of the bags and that she would need assistance transporting them to her room, she hugged me in mid-sentence before I could finish. "I am so grateful for whatever you've done! It's much more than we would have had otherwise," she said. "Well, let's get these gifts to your room," I said. "Merry Christmas!"

Even at my place of employment, I consider myself a "servant leader." I manage a team of four full-time employees (along with about a dozen contractor and part-time employees). I may be their direct supervisor, but I am not their "boss." They do not work for me; it is my pleasure to advocate for them. (1Timothy 3:1 NLT) Every woman on my team is an adult, first of all. They are wives, mothers, and grandmothers aside from being seasoned professionals (I am the youngest member of my team, unmarried, without children). They are the heads of their households; the "queen bees" of their own habitats… and I respect every bit of that when they step into their respective roles for our company.

I have as much to learn from them (if not more) as I strive to impart upon them. On our team, I have the most tenure in our organization; they possess the most life experiences. It's a beautiful synergistic relationship. I am responsible for not only rewarding them and honoring their work (i.e. yearly appraisals and salary increases) but I also have the charge of constructively and positively redirecting and correcting when appropriate.

And while it is much easier and more pleasant to lavish accolades and atta-girls, finding the right words to tell someone that something they said or did displeased a customer but now I need you to correct the mistake, never do it again and—oh! yeah—come back tomorrow ready to work and give it 100% is not. The process I take myself through is removing my own feelings from the situation. I ask myself: What do I want the overall outcome of this conversation to be? How will what I say be perceived by the recipient? How respectful can I be and cause the least amount of damage? And then I proceed with care. I am very fortunate to not have to have these conversations often. I serve an amazing team! Did I mention that I am also a member of a sorority whose mission is to be of "Service to All Mankind"? Yep. A "heart to serve" is who I am through and through.

I once heard a sermon about "Serving from the Saucer": Sometimes when you're given a cup of coffee or tea, a little saucer is placed underneath. If the cup overflows, the saucer will catch the excess; the cup contains more than it can hold. Once satisfied by the contents from the cup, one could drink the excess in the saucer or leave it behind to be discarded. Perhaps when God fills your cup—providing for all your needs—and excess flows over the sides into the saucer, you might consider serving others. He's done "exceeding abundantly!" (Ephesians 3:20) Atta Girl! Serve from the saucer - be it your time, your talents, your love, or your resources! Here's what I know that I know that I know:

"The thief cometh not, but for to steal, and to kill, and to
destroy: I am come that they might have life, ***and that they
might have it more abundantly.***" (John 10:10 NIV)
"Thou preparest a table before me in the presence of
mine enemies: thou anointest my head with oil,
my cup runneth over." (Psalm 23:5 NIV)
"For where your ***treasure*** is, there will your
heart be also." (Matthew 6:21 NIV)

God supplies all my needs. I am blessed to be a blessing. I have a heart to
serve. Cassandra is my name, and that is exactly who I am.

*Born in New Jersey, Cassandra is still a true
"Southern Girl" having lived in Montgomery
all her life. She began her career as an
elementary educator, a path that led her to
educational publishing & traveling across the
eastern U.S. supporting districts with at-risk
student populations. Living out of a suitcase
is commonplace for Cassandra as she enjoys
leisurely travel as well, especially to tropical climates. Regardless of her locale,
Cassandra believes firmly in the following: Faith, Family, Friends, and FUN!*

Walking in Your Calling

KATHY THOMAS MCFADDEN

According to Webster's Dictionary, "A calling is a strong inner impulse toward a particular course of action especially when accompanied by conviction of divine influences." Each one of us has a calling on our lives. For those in the ministry or doing spiritual work, there is a process of receiving, understanding and carrying out a person's call. In a general way a person's calling can also be described as a person's life purpose, mission or destiny.

It is an honor to be called by God and set aside for a specific purpose. Your calling is attached to your gifting in the body of Christ and your purpose in life. Most often it is a natural flow of who you are. To be called is from God and says that God trusts you with whatever God has called and created you to do. Because God called you, God will equip you, empower you and provide to you the resources, both spiritual and natural, to fulfill your calling. Walking in your calling is totally up to you.

Within the realms of your calling there will be many opportunities to walk in and walk out your calling. I believe people are waiting on and depending on those of us who have a calling on our lives to show up and to do what God has created and called us to do. Your calling is unique to you and to the body of Christ; it is needed and necessary in the larger scheme of things in the building of the Kingdom of God.

Walking in your calling is not always easy, but if God called you, it's doable and well worth it. There will be opposition and obstacles and times when you will be overlooked and overwhelmed and want to give up. There will be people who will oppose what you do and who you are; there will be obstacles within (fear, doubt, low self-esteem, etc.) and without (lack of resources, support and understanding).

There will be times when people will overlook you because you are a woman; and when it will feel like it is too much to deal with. And there will be times when you just want to give up and throw in the towel. But giving up is exactly what the enemy wants you to do, because more than you know, the enemy recognizes the calling on your life and the anointing and the power attached to your calling. The enemy realizes that every time you walk in your calling, exercise your gifting, use your authority, and refuse to back down, you make things happen; lives are transformed, and people are blessed.

My journey has not always been an easy one. It has had the remnants of a brewing quiet storm with something always lurking in the distance or behind the scenes. I serve as the first female pastor of the oldest African American church in Montgomery, Alabama; I have been appointed as the first female Presiding Elder of a District (overseeing 16 churches) in the A.M.E. Zion church, previously held by someone for forty-one years. I serve at every level in my denomination in many capacities. I love what I do; I know that I am called to do what I do and I know that God made room for my gifts in order for me to do what I do. But what I do in the spotlight, does not come without its struggles, both internally and externally. But by the grace of God, God gives me the strength and the encouragement to press on towards the higher calling in Christ Jesus.

I am encouraged by the women in the Bible such as Esther and Deborah, who with a holy boldness did what they were called to do with courage, a holy audacity, and without fear. Esther could be heard saying to Mordecai (after he reminded her that perhaps she was called to the kingdom of God for such a time as this), "If I perish, let me perish." Be encouraged! If God called you, God will not let you perish. Be encouraged that even if the weapon is formed against you (and it will be), it will not prosper!

I am also encouraged by women such as Michelle Obama, Oprah and Maxine Waters who have endured ridicule, judgment and criticism and have succeeded against the odds. They came from modest backgrounds and each one has excelled in what God has called them to do. Michelle Obama is the first African American woman to serve as the First Lady of the United States and has written a bestseller; Oprah has built a multi-million-dollar media empire and Maxine Waters has stood her ground on several occasions in Congress amongst some of the most powerful men in the country.

There will always be those who don't think you deserve what you have or where you are; who think that you are not good enough, smart enough or talented and gifted enough to do what you do and who will be jealous of what God has allowed you to do. But God thinks that you are deserving, good enough, smart enough, talented and gifted enough and fearfully and wonderfully made; and as long as you think so, you are well on your way to walking in your calling.

There are those who are watching near and far, for good and not so good reasons, to see what you are going to do with what God has entrusted you with. Some are cheering you on knowing that you have what it takes to succeed, and others are waiting for you to fail. Do not disappoint them! Be encouraged! Walk in your calling with your head held high, using every ounce of authority, anointing and power that God has given to you and go make a difference, go and make the world better, *"For the gifts and the calling of God are irrevocable."* (Romans 11:29 NKJV).

Kathy Thomas McFadden was born and raised in Washington, D.C. She holds a Bachelor of Arts degree. in Communications, a Master of Divinity and a Doctor of Ministry degree. She currently serves as the Pastor of Old Ship A.M.E. Zion Church in Montgomery. She made history when she was appointed in 2002 as its first female pastor in the church's 150-year history.

Dr. McFadden made history again when she was appointed as the first female Presiding Elder of The East Montgomery District, Central Alabama Conference in the Alabama-Florida Episcopal District. She is the Dean for Leadership Education and the Episcopal Director for Spiritual Formation for The Alabama-Florida Episcopal District of The A.M.E. Zion Church and Executive Director of The 400 Years Celebration, Inc. She is the CEO of MYQ Enterprises, which focuses on personal transformation and professional development.

"So are YOU ready to give birth?

I think you'll agree with me that the Women of God in this first volume are indeed examples of courage, faith, and grace who have shared their testimonies to the strengthening of others. As I was editing each sister's story, my mind thought about who I know them to be . . . and in every case, I was still surprised and blessed by something in their article. That just let me know that even though we might know people, there are still truths to learn about them and power to gain from hearing their true testimony.

This is the first volume of the series, and I am already praying that Women (and Men) of God will continue to allow their lives to be the rich ground from which life & healing springs in others. If YOU have a testimony, I encourage you to share it. Find a place that feels safe to you. Seek out people who honor you for the person you are & the life you've lived without judgement or hypocrisy. Tell your story. It will can & will give life.

A special God Bless You to all the amazing Women of God who agreed without hesitation to contribute to this work. They trusted the gifts of God in me & poured out their own truth to share with all of us. Thank You, My Anointed Sisters.

In Love, W. R. Coleman

Wendy R. Coleman is the 3ʳᵈ daughter of Mr. & Mrs. Joseph & Ruby Coleman and shares this honor with her four sisters, Victoria, Mamie, Shabra, and Monica. Her additional bright lights are 7 nieces & nephews and 8 great-nieces & nephews. Her numerous spiritual children make her the most joyful mother in the universe. They make her life rich.

A veteran higher education practitioner, Wendy has taught at Albany State University and at her alma mater, Alabama State University. She currently serves as Associate Professor and chair for the Department of Theatre & Dance there. Never satisfied with doing just one thing at a time, this Woman of God also owns Sweet, Sweet Spirit Publishing & JRC Event Center. She shares a vision for Coleman's Taste restaurant with her sister Shabra and brother-in-love Maceo. They are trusting God for manifestation in due season.

Wendy accepted her calling into the ministry in 1996 and was blessed to witness and learn servant-ministry under Sr. Pastor & Co-Pastor Roosevelt & LaVerne Carter at First Monumental Faith Ministries in Albany, Georgia. She served as pastor of First Congregational Christian Church in Montgomery for 6 years. God's guiding led her to birth Reaching The Remnant Ministries in 2018 where God is showing abundant favor and miraculous advancement.

Other Published/Produced Works by W. R. Coleman

The Man of God: A Story about Forgiveness (Novel)
Born Again (Stage Play)
Let the Church Say . . . (Stage Play)

This is Our Story:
Learning, Loving, and Living Well with Diabetes
(Stage Play commissioned through the Bayer Dream Fund)

Printed in the United States
By Bookmasters